Contents

Bears

Birthdays

BUNNIES, BEARS, AND BIRTHDAYS

BY MARTI ABBOTT AND BETTY JANE POLK

FEARON TEACHER AIDS
Simon & Schuster Supplementary Education Group

Editor: Carol Williams
Copyeditor: Cynthia Seagren
Illustration: Tom McFarland
Design: Diann Abbott

ISBN 0-8224-0638-1

Printed in the United States of America
1. 9 8 7 6 5 4 3 2 1

Introduction

All too often teachers read a book to children to entertain them or fill some spare moments, and that is the end of it. With the closing of the book, teachers shut out children's responses and ideas. Teachable moments are lost forever. The Books and Beyond series provides teachers with creative activities and critical-thinking stimulators to maximize the effectiveness of good literature. A piece of literature can become the basis for a learning unit that spans many areas of the curriculum.

Each lesson in the Books and Beyond series begins with a brief synopsis of the book and introductory ideas to stimulate student interest. After reading the book aloud, the use of the critical-thinking and discussion questions will help children draw from their own related experiences and analyze, evaluate, and apply the message of the book. Follow-up activities that center around many curriculum areas and include a variety of teaching styles will help children move beyond the book and internalize its message.

Bunnies, Bears, and Birthdays is a collection of lessons based on children's books that deal with furry friends and celebrations. A blend of fact and fiction, the lessons provide children with opportunities to use their imaginations, inventiveness, and reasoning abilities. Children create art projects, make maps, conduct scientific experiments, compose original poems, and even learn a new song or two. The familiar topics of bunnies, bears, and birthdays provide a perfect springboard to launch your students into new areas of learning and growth.

Mr. Rabbit and the Lovely Present

Written by Charlotte Zolotow and illustrated by Maurice Sendak
New York: Harper & Row, 1962

Synopsis

A little girl asks Mr. Rabbit if he can give her some ideas for her mother's birthday gift. She tells Mr. Rabbit that her mother likes the colors red, yellow, green, and blue. Mr. Rabbit's first gift suggestions (a fire engine, a taxicab, and a lake) seem a bit impractical. But together, they finally do come up with the perfect birthday gift.

Introduction

Ask children if they have ever had trouble finding the perfect gift for a friend or family member. Encourage children to share some of their past gift ideas. Ask children what they think would be the perfect gift for a mother. Explain to the children that the little girl in the story has trouble deciding what the perfect gift would be for her mother, so she asks Mr. Rabbit for some advice. Invite the children to listen closely as the story is read aloud to find out how the little girl solves her problem.

Critical-Thinking and Discussion Questions

1. The little girl thought that she could solve her problem better if she asked for help. Do you ask for help when you have a problem? Have you ever felt like you wanted help, but there was no one to help you? When? Are there some problems that you would rather solve by yourself? What?
2. Why do you think the little girl went to Mr. Rabbit for help? Do you think he had successfully helped her solve other problems? Was he smart or was he the only one around? Who do you ask for help when you have a problem?
3. Have you ever had trouble figuring out what kind of gift to buy for someone? How did you solve the problem?
4. Do you think the little girl's mother will like the gift? Why or why not?
5. At the end of the story, Mr. Rabbit said that he was very glad to have been able to help the little girl. Are you like Mr. Rabbit in that way? Do you like to help people? When was the last time you helped someone? How did it make you feel?

Creative Writing Starters
Language Arts

My favorite color is _____ because it reminds me of _____ .
When you choose a gift for someone, you should _____ .
I usually ask for help from _____ when I need it.

Story Titles
The Perfect Present
A World Without Color
Rabbit's Response

The Perfect Gift
Language Arts

The little girl in *Mr. Rabbit and the Lovely Present* was in search of
the perfect gift for her mother. She wanted to find something that her
mother would like and would find useful. Invite children to brainstorm some perfect gifts for the following:

What would be a perfect gift for . . .
   a large grizzly bear?
   a child about to begin his or her first day at school?
   a small, playful puppy?
   a star basketball player?
   a person about to move to Hawaii?

After generating some ideas, give each child a copy of the "A Perfect
Gift for _____ " reproducible on page 13. Have each child think of
a name of a person or animal they would like to present with a birthday gift and fill in the blank in the title. Encourage children to write a
paragraph or short story explaining what the gift is and why it is so
appropriate for the person they chose.

Color Connection
Language Arts

Divide students into groups of three or four and give each group a copy of the "Color Connection" gameboard on page 14, a die, and game markers. Cut several small squares of red, yellow, green, and blue construction paper and put them in a paper lunch sack for each group. The first player rolls the die and then reaches in the paper sack and pulls out a colored square. The player must name something that is the same color as the square. The player then moves his or her marker the number of spaces on the gameboard indicated by the die. Play continues clockwise until one player reaches "The Perfect Gift." To make the game more challenging, do not allow players to repeat items that have already been mentioned. The group can keep track of named items by folding a sheet of paper into four columns and labeling each column with one of the four colors. Have players keep a written list of each colored item mentioned by listing it in the appropriate column on the paper.

Color Collage
Art

Walk past each child's desk, saying a color to each child as you pass. Encourage the child you pass to name something the color you mention as quickly as possible. Then invite each child to choose his or her favorite color and make a color collage using only that color. Provide construction paper, yarn, glitter, paint, and scraps of fabric.

Fruit Fun

Health

Ask the children what they think the little girl's mother did with her basket of fruit. Suggest that she may have cut the fruit up to make a salad. Cut up several green pears, bananas, and red apples. Add some grapes to make a fruit salad. Share the salad with the class and discuss some of the health benefits of eating fruit:

> Pears, apples, and bananas contain vitamin A, which helps maintain healthy skin and eyes. The apples and bananas contain vitamin C, which helps wounds heal. Grapes have a high sugar content, which makes them a good source of energy.

Encourage children to share other ways they know of to prepare these four types of fruit. Take it a step further by asking children to research and find out some interesting facts about these four types of fruit. Provide the following examples to spark interest.

> People in the United States eat about 11 billion bananas a year.
> Pears ripen best *after* they are removed from the tree.
> Apples are 85 percent water.
> Grapes can be black, blue, golden, green, red, purple, or white.

A Perfect Gift for

_____

Write a description of the gift you would like to give.
Tell why the gift would be perfect.

_____
_____
_____
_____
_____
_____
_____
_____
_____
_____
_____
_____
_____
_____

Color Connection

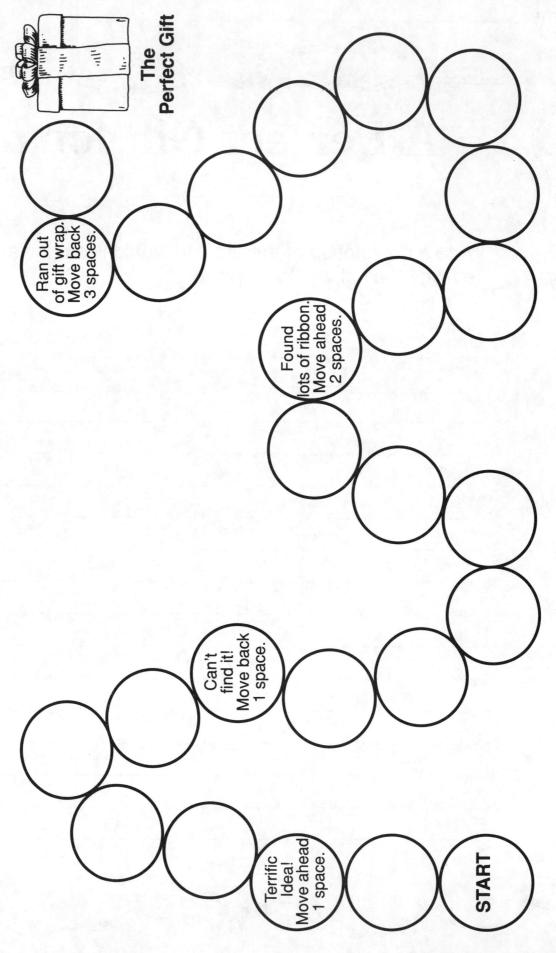

The Perfect Gift

Ran out of gift wrap. Move back 3 spaces.

Found lots of ribbon. Move ahead 2 spaces.

Can't find it! Move back 1 space.

Terrific Idea! Move ahead 1 space.

START

Mr. Rabbit and the Lovely Present

Bunnies, Bears, and Birthdays © 1991 Fearon Teacher Aids

Who's in Rabbit's House

Written by Verna Aardema and illustrated by Leo and Diane Dillon
New York: Dial Press, 1969

Synopsis

In this Masai tale, Rabbit is unable to get into her house because The Long One is inside and threatens to trample her. Several animal friends offer suggestions for getting The Long One out of the house, but Rabbit finds the suggestions unsuitable. The problem is finally solved with the help of someone Rabbit initially thought was incapable of helping.

Introduction

Ask children what they do when they have a problem. Encourage children to share problem-solving techniques that have been successful, as well as some that have not worked. Explain to children that Rabbit has a problem in the story—someone is in her house. Invite the children to listen closely as the story is read aloud to find out how Rabbit solves her problem.

Critical-Thinking and Discussion Questions

1. Rabbit sat down on a nearby log to think when she first realized she had a problem. What do you usually do when you have a problem? How do you go about solving it? Do you try to think of a solution by yourself or do you usually ask someone for help?
2. Rabbit was not willing to accept help from Frog. How do you think that made Frog feel? What would you have done if you were Frog? Has anyone ever rejected an idea of yours or refused to let you help them? How did you feel?
3. Jackal, Leopard, Elephant, and Rhinoceros each had a different idea for getting The Long One out of Rabbit's house, but all of the ideas would have destroyed Rabbit's home. Can you think of an idea (besides Frog's) that would have gotten The Long One out without destroying the house? What would you have suggested to Rabbit?
4. Why do you think the caterpillar went into Rabbit's house in the first place? Do you think Rabbit would have let the caterpillar live in the house if the caterpillar had asked instead of just taking over the house? Why or why not?
5. How do you think the relationship between Rabbit and Frog changed from the beginning of the story to the end? Do you think Frog will offer to help Rabbit with a future problem? Do you think Rabbit will accept Frog's help next time?

15

Creative Writing Starters
Language Arts

When I have a problem I usually _____ .
The best advice I ever gave was when _____ .
If someone didn't like my idea, I would _____ .

Story Titles
The Perfect Plan
Mystery Guest
The Frog Who Couldn't Stop Laughing

Animal Masks
Language Arts and Art

Write the names of the seven characters from the story on the chalkboard. Divide the class into groups of seven. Have each group cooperatively assign one character from the story to each group member. Give each child a large paper grocery bag cut to shoulder length to design a mask for his or her character. Help the children mark and cut out eye holes in the paper bags. Encourage creativity and inventiveness. Provide a variety of materials, such as construction paper, fabric, wallpaper scraps, buttons, cardboard tubes, and plastic containers. After children have completed their masks, review the story and the actions of each character. Make some notes on the chalkboard next to each character's name. Invite children to work together in their groups to organize a dramatic presentation of the story using their masks. Give each group an opportunity to perform for the class.

Ideophones
Language Arts

The author used ideophones in the story *Who's in Rabbit's House* to produce rhythmic sounds, which are often present in African tales. Point out and review some of the ideophones from the story:

    banging on the door—ban, ban, ban
    Frog crouching—semm
    bits of roof flying off—zzt, zzt, zzt
    Rabbit smoothing roof—bet, bet, bet
    Frog laughing aloud—gdung, gdung, gdung

Give each child a copy of the "Ideophones" reproducible on page 18. Invite children to create an original ideophone for each action and then use some of the actions and ideophones in a short paragraph describing a typical day at school.

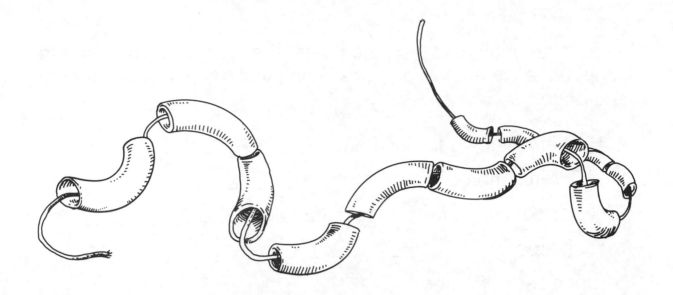

Masai Macaroni Necklaces
Art

The Masai wore colorful necklaces as depicted in the opening illustrations in *Who's in Rabbit's House.* Dye macaroni various colors by combining $1/2$ cup rubbing alcohol with $1/2$ tablespoon of food coloring in glass bowls. Put two cups of macaroni in each color mixture. Stir the macaroni in the coloring until it is well-coated and then dip it out of the solution. Spread the macaroni on newspaper to dry for about ten minutes. Put a piece of tape on one end of a yarn string for each child and invite the children to string the colorful macaroni to make beautiful necklaces.

Where Is Rabbit's House?
Social Studies

The story, *Who's in Rabbit's House,* takes place in Africa. Ask children to think of some things they noticed in the story that were different from their own environment and culture. They may have noticed that Rabbit's house looked very different from their houses or that wild animals were roaming freely. Use this opportunity to compare and contrast African environment and culture with your own. Point out Africa on a world map and discuss its relationship to where you live.

Name _____

Ideophones

Create an original ideophone for each action. Use some of the ideophones in a short paragraph on the lines at the bottom of the page.

1. basketball going through hoop _____

2. children jumping rope _____

3. water coming out of drinking fountain _____

4. footsteps _____

5. lunch sack opening _____

6. crayons marking on paper _____

7. chalk writing on chalkboard _____

8. book closing _____

9. children whispering _____

10. pencil being sharpened _____

_____

_____

_____

_____

_____

_____

_____

_____

Bunnies, Bears, and Birthdays © 1991 Fearon Teacher Aids

Who's in Rabbit's House

Little Rabbit's Loose Tooth

Written by Lucy Bate and illustrated by Diane DeGroat
New York: Crown Publishers, 1975

Synopsis

When Little Rabbit loses a tooth while eating chocolate ice cream, she discovers that she has a window in her mouth that she can stick her tongue through. After some creative thought and much debate about what to do with her tooth, she finally decides to leave it under her pillow for the tooth fairy.

Introduction

Ask children what they do (or will do) with a tooth when they lose it. Many children may say they will leave it under their pillow for the tooth fairy. Ask children if they can think of some other things to do with a loose tooth. Invite children to listen closely as the story is read aloud to find out what Little Rabbit does with her loose tooth.

Critical-Thinking and Discussion Questions

1. Little Rabbit was worried that some foods would be too hard for her to eat when she had a loose tooth. If you had a loose tooth, which foods would you think would be too hard to eat? Which soft foods would you eat?
2. While Little Rabbit was eating chocolate ice cream, her tooth finally fell out. What were you doing the last time you lost a tooth? What did you do with the tooth?
3. Little Rabbit was not sure she wanted to leave her tooth for the tooth fairy. She began to think of some other ways to use her tooth. Can you think of a creative way to use a tooth? If you chose not to leave your tooth for the tooth fairy, what would *you* do with it?
4. Little Rabbit's mother told Little Rabbit that the tooth fairy might leave a dime in exchange for the tooth. How much money do you think a tooth is worth?
5. Little Rabbit made some guesses about what the tooth fairy might do with all those teeth she collects. What do you think she does with them?
6. What do you think Little Rabbit will do with the dime the tooth fairy left? What do you usually do with money you receive? Do you save it or spend it? What do you like to buy?

Creative Writing Starters
Language Arts

When I lose a tooth, I will _____ .
It would be difficult to eat _____ with a loose tooth.
I think the tooth fairy _____ .

Story Titles
The Window in My Mouth
Tooth Fairy Trouble
The Million-Dollar Tooth

My Wiggly Tooth
Language Arts

After hearing Little Rabbit's story about losing her first tooth, children will undoubtedly be excited to share a loose-tooth experience with the class. Students may choose to share about the first tooth they lost, what they did with one of their teeth, or what they hope the tooth fairy will leave under their pillow when they lose their very first tooth. Tape record each child's story. Play the stories back for the class or make the tape available at an audio learning center. Children love to hear themselves speak and will enjoy hearing the stories over and over. The experience can also be turned into an opportunity to improve oral communication skills. Children will be quick to point out their own errors and may even want to try telling the stories again.

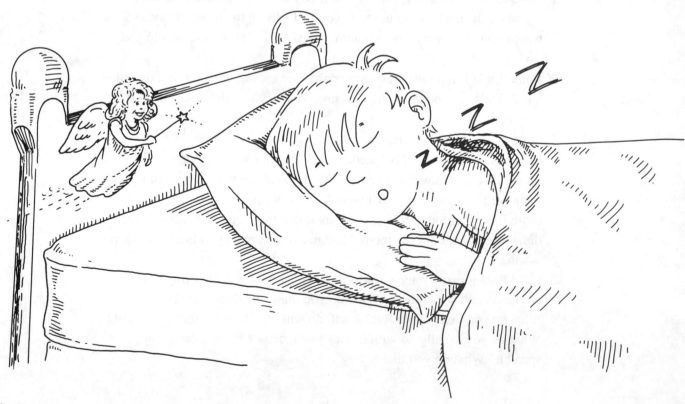

Tooth Chart
Science

Give each child a copy of the "Tooth Chart" reproducible on page 23. Explain the name and purpose of each of the deciduous teeth.

> *Incisors* are the chief biting teeth. They have a sharp, straight cutting edge.
>
> *Canines* are also used to bite. They can be used to tear off pieces of food.
>
> *Molars* are used to crush and grind food. They have a broad, lumpy top instead of a sharp biting edge. The small surface lumps are called *cusps*.

Provide mirrors if possible and encourage children to identify the molars, canines, and incisors in their mouths. Invite children to fill in the blanks at the bottom of the reproducible. Children can draw an X through the teeth in the diagram that they have lost.

Tooth Tallies
Math

Make a bar graph on the chalkboard or a chart to represent the tallies for lost teeth among class members. Use the horizontal axis for the number of teeth lost and the vertical axis for the number of children that have lost a particular number of teeth. After children have calculated by looking in the mirror how many teeth they have lost, begin the graphing process. Ask children who have never lost a tooth to stand. Count the number of standing children and color in one box on the graph for each child in the "0" column. Ask those children to sit down and ask for children who have lost one tooth to stand. Color in a box for each of these standing children in the "1" column. Continue until all children have stood one time and a box is colored in on the graph to represent each child. When the graph is complete, ask children some questions, such as:

> How many children have lost three teeth?
> How many children have never lost a tooth?
> How many teeth have been lost in the whole class all together?

The Disappearing Tooth
Health

Invite a school nurse or dental health educator to come visit the class and talk about dental health. Provide a demonstration on proper brushing and flossing techniques. Remind children that the food we eat and our brushing habits influence the amount of plaque that builds up on our teeth. Demonstrate how a disclosing tablet works to help locate areas of our teeth that need better care. To demonstrate how sugary substances can harm our teeth if we do not brush properly, put a real tooth in a plastic glass or bottle filled with a cola drink. After several days, the tooth will dissolve. After the discussion of good dental hygiene, give each child a copy of the "Happy Tooth" reproducible on page 24. Encourage children to write down three good dental health rules they will try to remember to keep their teeth healthy and strong.

Tooth Chart

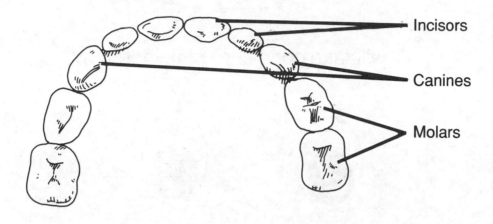

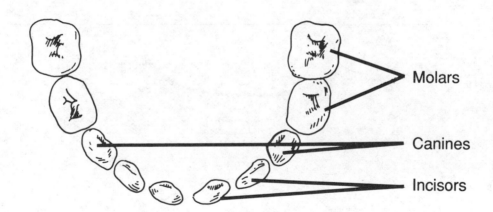

I have lost _____ teeth.

I have _____ teeth in my mouth now.

Name _____

Happy Tooth

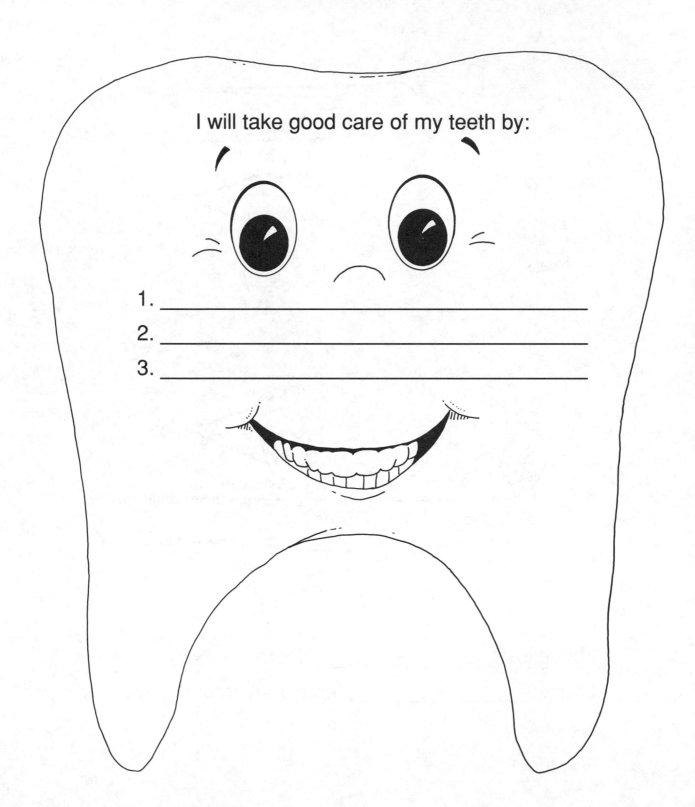

I will take good care of my teeth by:

1. _____
2. _____
3. _____

Bunnies, Bears, and Birthdays © 1991 Fearon Teacher Aids

The Runaway Bunny

Written by Margaret Wise Brown and illustrated by Clement Hurd
New York: Harper & Row, 1972

Synopsis

Little bunny tells his mother he is going to run away and then plans creative ways to escape his mother's presence. But each time, his mother comes up with an equally inventive plan to be near her little bunny. In the end, little bunny realizes that he might as well stay where he belongs—and so he happily does.

Introduction

Ask the children if they have ever felt like getting away someplace where no one could find them or tell them what to do. Explain to the children that the little bunny in the story thinks of creative ways to hide from his mother. Encourage children to listen closely as the story is read aloud to find out if the little bunny successfully runs away from his mother.

Critical-Thinking and Discussion Questions

1. Why do you think the little bunny wanted to run away? Have you ever wanted to run away? Why? Do you think running away solves problems? Why or why not?
2. Do you think there is anything the little bunny could have chosen to become so that his mother would not have been able to find him? If so, what?
3. Do you think the little bunny would have been happy if he had finally found a way to run away from his mother without her finding him? Why or why not?
4. Why do you think the mother was so persistent about finding the bunny each time he told how he would hide from her? Who would try to find you no matter what?
5. How do you think the bunny felt about his mother always wanting to be near him? How does it make you feel when someone wants to be near you and care for you?

Creative Writing Starters
Language Arts

If I ran away, I would become a _____ so no one could find me.
If I ran away, my family would _____ .
I know _____ cares for me because _____ .

Story Titles
The Perfect Hideaway
Runaway Rescue
No Place to Hide

If You Are, I Will Be
Language Arts

Ask children to think about some other things little bunny might have thought about being to hide from his mother. List some of the ideas on the chalkboard and then ask children to think of what the mother bunny would have become in each case. For example, if little bunny would have said, "I will be a car and drive away," mother bunny might have said, "Then, I will be a red traffic light to make you stop." After discussing some ideas and examples, give each child a copy of the "Runaway Bunny" reproducible on page 28. Encourage each child to think of something bunny could be and then an equally clever idea for what mother bunny might become in response. Invite children to illustrate their ideas. Combine all the pages together to make a class book.

Song of the Runaway Bunny
Music

Margaret Wise Brown has written the lyrics for "Song of the Runaway Bunny" printed in the back of *The Runaway Bunny* book. Learn the song along with the children and sing it as a lullaby. Encourage children to add some hand motions or body movements as they sing.

Dough Bunnies
Art

Mix two parts flour and one part salt. Add enough water to make an easy-to-handle dough. Give each child a ball of dough and encourage children to make a bunny of their own. Discuss some distinguishing features of a bunny, such as long hind feet and long ears. After the dough figures have dried (it will take several days, or you can speed the process by drying the figures in a very low-temperature oven), invite the children to paint the bunnies and glue on a cotton tail.

Bunny Trivia
Science

Have children point out aspects that make *The Runaway Bunny* a make-believe story. Ask children to pretend that they are going to write a *true* story about a bunny. Encourage children to think about some facts they know about bunnies, such as what they eat, where they live, and what they are able to do. Correct any misconceptions children may have about bunnies and add to their knowledge by discussing the following bunny trivia:

Bunnies do not walk or run. They move about by hopping.

When chased, a bunny can hop as fast as 18 miles per hour.

A bunny can see things behind or to the side of it because a bunny's eyes are on the side of its head.

Most bunnies live in shallow holes called *forms*.

Most bunnies eat and play from dusk to dawn and spend the rest of the day resting and sleeping.

People are the bunny's greatest enemy.

A frightened bunny can leap 10 feet.

Name _____

Runaway Bunny

"I will be a _____ and _____,"
    said little bunny.

"Then I will be a _____ and _____,"
    said mother bunny.

Bunnies, Bears, and Birthdays © 1991 Fearon Teacher Aids

The Velveteen Rabbit

Written by Margery Williams and illustrated by William Nicholson
New York: Doubleday, 1975

Synopsis

The Velveteen Rabbit, one of many forgotten toys on the nursery shelf, longs to become Real. The wise old Skin Horse explains that becoming Real happens only when a child really loves you. It can sometimes hurt and it takes a long time. The Velveteen Rabbit does become Real and finds the experience everything the Skin Horse said it would be—and more.

Introduction

Ask children to tell about one of their favorite stuffed animals. Ask children to imagine that this stuffed animal comes to life. Encourage children to imagine the adventures they could have with their "real" stuffed animals. Explain to children that the Velveteen Rabbit has hopes of becoming "real" someday. Invite children to listen closely as the story is read aloud to find out what it takes to make the Velveteen Rabbit "real."

Critical-Thinking and Discussion Questions

1. What did the Skin Horse tell the Velveteen Rabbit about what it meant to become Real? Which of your toys have you loved enough to be Real?

2. How do you think the Velveteen Rabbit felt when he was talking to and comparing himself with real rabbits? Have you ever compared yourself to someone else and felt less important or not as good? When? Why did you feel that way?

3. In the story, the Skin Horse says that the nursery magic is "strange and wonderful." What strange and wonderful magic would you like to happen to you or one of your toys?

4. The Skin Horse was wise because he had lived longer than any of the others. Do you think people who are older are wiser? Do you think you are wise? What do you think will make you wiser?

5. How do you think the Velveteen Rabbit felt after he had been made Real at the end of the story? Do you think he wished he could once again be the Boy's favorite stuffed rabbit? Why or why not?

Creative Writing Starters
Language Arts

I wish my _____ could become real.
If the nursery magic Fairy visited me, I would ask her to _____ .
I think becoming real means _____.

Story Titles
Becoming Real
Shabby and Torn
The Toy That Came Alive

Toy Thoughts
Language Arts

The thoughts and feelings of the Velveteen Rabbit that lead to his becoming Real are clearly expressed in the story. The following passage from the story is a good example of how a stuffed toy might feel about a very commonplace occurrence:

> ". . . the Velveteen Rabbit slept in the Boy's bed. At first he found it rather uncomfortable, for the Boy hugged him very tight, and sometimes he rolled over on him, and sometimes he pushed him so far under the pillow that the Rabbit could scarcely breathe."

Encourage children to imagine how one of their stuffed toys or dolls might feel if they could express themselves. Give each child a sheet of lined writing paper. Encourage each child to choose one toy and write a short paragraph or a story from that toy's perspective.

Descriptive Differences
Language Arts

The Boy used to take the Velveteen Rabbit out to the nearby woods with him. One day the Velveteen Rabbit met some rabbits like himself. But upon closer examination, he noticed some differences between himself and these furry animals. Reread the passage in *The Velveteen Rabbit* that describes this scene in the woods. Ask children to name the differences between a real rabbit and a stuffed rabbit that were mentioned in the story and to add some of their own. Give each child a copy of the "Descriptive Differences" reproducible on page 32. Encourage each child to draw a picture of a real rabbit and a stuffed rabbit. Invite children to describe each rabbit on the lines provided.

Bunny Basket
Art

Have each child bring a half-gallon milk carton from home that is rinsed out and clean. Open the spout and lay each carton on its side with the spout up. Cut off the spout and the long side panel that is facing up. Cut a $1/2$" long strip from the panel that has been cut away. Give each child the prepared carton and the $1/2$" strip. Have children staple the strip to each side of the carton to make a handle for the basket. Invite children to cover the entire carton by gluing on cotton balls. Encourage children to decorate the pointed end of the carton to look like a bunny's face by gluing on construction paper ears, eyes, nose, and whiskers.

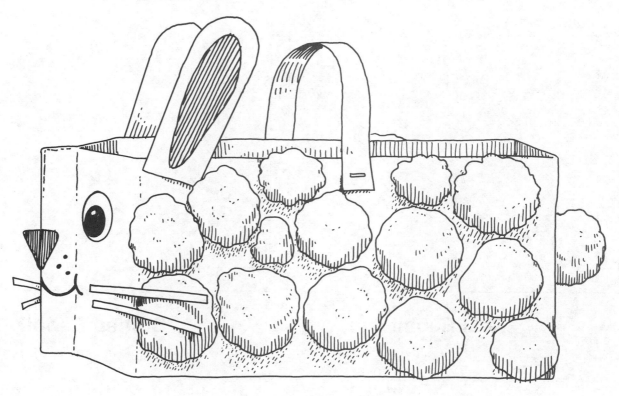

Pet Care
Science

Discuss the difference in the care the Velveteen Rabbit received and the care a real rabbit should receive. Discuss proper care of pets. Ask students to tell about pets they have and what they do to care for their pets. Invite each student to choose a pet they have or would like to have and do some research to find out some important do's and don'ts for the care of their pets. When the research is complete, encourage students to share the information with the class. Students can make posters or charts to help communicate their pet care findings.

Name _____

Descriptive Differences

Draw a picture of a real rabbit and a stuffed rabbit in the boxes below. Describe each rabbit on the lines below each picture.

Real Rabbit

Stuffed Rabbit

_____   _____

_____   _____

_____   _____

_____   _____

_____   _____

_____   _____

_____   _____

Bunnies, Bears, and Birthdays © 1991 Fearon Teacher Aids

Listen, Rabbit

Written by Aileen Fisher and illustrated by Symeon Shimin
New York: Thomas Y. Crowell, 1964

Synopsis

A poetic account of a young boy who seeks the friendship of a rabbit. The boy studies the rabbit's habits as he carefully observes him throughout the seasons of the year. When spring finally arrives, a wonderful surprise awaits the patient boy.

Introduction

Ask the children what kind of wild animal they would choose for a pet, if they had their choice. Explain to the children that the little boy in this story chooses to make a wild rabbit his friend, but he runs into some obstacles. Invite the children to listen closely as the story is read aloud to find out how the boy goes about building a friendship with this wild rabbit.

Critical-Thinking and Discussion Questions

1. When the boy first saw the rabbit out in the field, he was not sure what it was. What might you expect to see in a field? What made the boy finally realize it was a rabbit?
2. The boy knew that he needed to be very still and quiet when he was around the rabbit so he would not scare it. What else do you think the boy could have done to make friends with the rabbit? What would you have done?
3. Do you think the rabbit understood that the boy wanted to be friends? Why are wild animals afraid of people? Should they be?
4. The boy seemed to be very patient and did not give up hope that the rabbit would be his friend. Summer, fall, and winter passed and the boy kept trying. What does it mean to be patient? Have you ever waited a really long time to get something you wanted? What was it? Were you patient?
5. The boy pondered some of the amazing features of the rabbit, such as his keen sense of hearing, his quick feet, and his smartly placed eyes. What do you think the rabbit might have been thinking about the boy's body? What do you think is amazing about the way your body is made? What are some things you can do that a rabbit cannot do?
6. Do you think the little boy will get a chance to be friends with the baby rabbits? Why or why not?

Creative Writing Starters
Language Arts

The best way to make friends is to _____ .
If I could have any pet I wanted, I would choose a _____ .
Wild animals are _____ .

Story Titles
Antennae Ears
Cottontail Babies
Friends Forever

Poetic Possibilities
Language Arts

Discuss the author's use of poetry as she told the story of the little boy and the rabbit. Reread some of the pages and ask children to point out the rhyming words. Make a list of the words on the chalkboard. Choose a group of rhyming words from the list and compose an original class poem together. Give each child a sheet of lined paper and encourage children to choose a group of rhyming words and write a short poem individually. Children can illustrate their poems after they have been edited and recopied. Display the poems on a bulletin board or combine them together in a class book.

Profile Perspectives
Art

When the little boy first saw the rabbit, he could only see one eye bulging out from the side of his head. Show the children the picture in *Listen, Rabbit* that illustrates this first meeting. Ask children why the boy only saw one eye. Invite the children to look closely at the picture of the boy and observe that the boy only has one eye and one ear in the drawing. Introduce the word *profile* to the students and help them to see that people, objects, and animals look different from a sideways perspective than they do straight on. Make a profile silhouette drawing of each child. Shine a bright light against a wall. Have each child sit in a chair sideways against a wall with the light shining brightly on them so their profile is outlined on the wall. Hold a sheet of construction paper up on the wall and, using a pencil, trace the child's silhouette. Give each child his or her profile to cut out. Children can add details using crayons or markers to complete their profile pictures.

Did You Know?
Science

The boy in *Listen, Rabbit* wanted very badly for the rabbit to listen to
him and become his friend. Our ears provide us with the ability to
hear what is going on around us. Encourage children to share any information they know about our ears and how they work. Give each
child a copy of the "Did You Know..." reproducible on page 36.
Have students cut the four pages apart and stack them in order to
make a booklet. Give each child a piece of colored construction
paper for the front and back covers of the booklet. Students can title
their booklets "Did You Know?" Read the information on each page
to the students as they follow along in their own booklets, or invite
students to read the information independently. Have the students
draw a picture on each page illustrating the text.

Antennae Ears
Science

The little boy in *Listen, Rabbit* took special note of the rabbit's ears.
In fact, the shape of the rabbit's ear helped the boy identify that the
animal he saw from afar was a rabbit. The little boy said, "Listen,
rabbit, with such tall ears, you hear more than *anyone* hears." The
little boy wished that he had antennae ears like the rabbit so he could
hear all the sounds that people cannot normally hear. Give children
an opportunity to use their sense of hearing to identify sounds they
hear everyday. Make a tape recording of familiar sounds, such as a
door slamming, a doorbell ringing, a telephone busy signal, a blow
dryer, and water running in the sink. Play one sound at a time from
the tape and ask children to identify each sound they hear.

Did You Know . . .

that your ears help you balance?
Draw a picture of yourself doing a
balancing act. Don't forget to draw
your ears!

1

Did You Know . . .

that some animals can close their
ears? A seal can close its ears
when it dives underwater. Draw a
seal diving underwater.

2

Did You Know . . .

that the loudness of sounds is
measured on a special scale
called decibels? A soft sound like
a whisper is only 20 decibels.
Draw a picture of a soft sound.

3

Did You Know . . .

that a normal conversation
measures 60 decibels and a very
loud noise like a jet plane taking
off measures 160 decibels. Draw
a picture of a very loud sound.

4

Foolish Rabbit's Big Mistake

Written by Rafe Martin and illustrated by Ed Young
New York: G.P. Putnam's Sons, 1985

Synopsis

This Jataka tale is one of the oldest versions of "Henny Penny" or "The Sky Is Falling." Foolish rabbit quickly jumps to the conclusion that the earth is breaking up when an apple falls to the ground beside him. He spreads the news and gathers a crowd of frantic followers. The brave lion puts a stop to the chaos by making the animals face their unrealistic fears.

Introduction

Ask children if they have ever made a mistake and to describe how they felt. Reassure children that everyone makes mistakes and that mistakes are often a good way for us to learn an important lesson. Invite children to listen closely as the story is read aloud to find out what mistake the rabbit makes and what lesson he learns from it.

Critical-Thinking and Discussion Questions

1. Many of the animals believed what the rabbit told them about the earth breaking up. They immediately ran and followed the rabbit. One animal, the lion, questioned whether the rabbit was right. How would you have responded if the rabbit had told you the news about the earth breaking up? Why?

2. A rumor is information that is spread without full knowledge of its accuracy. What do you do with information that you receive from others? Do you find out if it is true or do you just pass it along to the next person?

3. The animals who believed that the earth was truly breaking up were very frightened. They began to run. Have you ever felt very frightened? What frightened you? What did you do?

4. The lion helped the rabbit to see his mistake. The rabbit then had to go back and tell the others he had been wrong. The other animals were angry with the rabbit for telling them something that wasn't true. What do you do when you realize you have made a mistake? How do you feel when someone else tells you they have made a mistake? Do you know anyone who has *never* made a mistake? Do you think it is OK to make mistakes?

5. The rabbit's fear disappeared when he stopped to look at what was frightening him. What can you learn from the rabbit's foolish mistake?

Creative Writing Starters

Language Arts

I was very frightened when _____ .
Someone once told me _____ and so I _____ .
When I make a mistake, I _____ .

Story Titles
My Big Mistake
Earth Shattering News
The Secret That Soon Spread

Comparison Study

Language Arts

After reading the story, give each student a copy of "The Big Mistake" reproducible on page 40. Invite students to fill in the information from *Foolish Rabbit's Big Mistake* on the form. Obtain copies of similar stories ("Henny Penny," "Chicken Little," or "The Sky Is Falling") to do a comparison study. Read the stories aloud to the children and then ask them to find similarities and differences. Or, divide children into groups to read the stories to each other. Provide children with more copies of "The Big Mistake" reproducible to fill in the information from the other versions of the story. Encourage students to write their own stories using the same basic elements.

Story Sequence
Language Arts

Divide the class into groups of nine. Give each group a copy of the "Story Sequence" reproducible on page 41. Ask each group to cut the sentence strips apart and distribute one strip to each group member. Encourage each group member to read his or her sentence strip aloud. After all sentences have been read, invite groups to cooperatively organize each member in line so when the sentence strips are read again, they are in the proper sequence. Invite each group to read their retelling of *Foolish Rabbit's Big Mistake* in front of the class. After each group has organized their story in the proper sequence, have groups number the sentence strips. Give each child a 9" x 12" sheet of construction paper. Have each student glue his or her sentence strip on the paper and then illustrate it. Combine each group's sentences together in a booklet.

Is the Earth Breaking Up?
Science

Foolish rabbit thought the earth was breaking up when he heard the crash made by an apple falling to the ground. Invite students to do some research on earthquakes to find out the answers to the following questions:

Why do earthquakes occur?
Can earthquakes be predicted?
What should you do to prepare for an earthquake?
Where are earthquakes most likely to occur?
How is the intensity of an earthquake measured?

Divide students into groups to do research or assign individual projects.

Math Mistakes
Math

The lion pointed out that the foolish rabbit had made a big mistake. Discuss with the children how everyone makes mistakes and that steps can be taken to correct a mistake. Give each child a copy of the "Math Mistakes" reproducible on page 42. Have children cut apart the worksheet on the dotted line. Invite children to find and cut out the four math problems that have incorrect answers and glue them in the "mistake" boxes. Have children rework the problems and provide the correct answers in the "correction" boxes.

Name _____

The Big Mistake

Carefully read and answer each question.

Story Title: _____

1. Who was the main character? _____

2. What frightened the main character? _____

_____

_____

3. What did the main character think was happening? _____

_____

_____

4. Who did the main character tell the news to? _____

_____

_____

5. How was the big mistake cleared up? _____

_____

_____

Bunnies, Bears, and Birthdays © 1991 Fearon Teacher Aids

Story Sequence

Cut the sentence strips apart. Put them in the correct order to retell the story of *Foolish Rabbit's Big Mistake.*

"Raarrggh!" roared the lion. "Why are you all running? The earth is not breaking up!"
The elephant charged off with the others as the terrified animals shouted the news.
The rabbits told the bears that the earth was breaking up. The bears joined the other frightened animals as they ran for their lives.
The rabbit explained his mistake to the other animals.
Little rabbit heard a crash behind him and he ran to warn everyone.
The lion advised the animals that they should find out what is frightening them next time. They might find out that there is nothing to be afraid of at all.
The snake came sliding to join the animals when it heard the news.
When little rabbit shouted the news to other rabbits he passed by, they began running, too.
The rabbit jumped on the lion's back as they went back to the apple tree to find out what had frightened the rabbit.

Math Mistakes

Cut apart the worksheet on the dotted line. Cut out and glue the four math problems that have incorrect answers in the boxes labeled "mistake." Correct the mistakes by redoing each math problem in the "correction" boxes.

Mistake	**Correction**	**Mistake**	**Correction**

Mistake	**Correction**	**Mistake**	**Correction**

$$426 \atop +94$$
___
$$420$$

$$147 \atop -\ 32$$
___
$$115$$

$$353 \atop +112$$
___
$$465$$

$$278 \atop -102$$
___
$$176$$

$$564 \atop -231$$
___
$$233$$

$$286 \atop +113$$
___
$$399$$

$$153 \atop +462$$
___
$$515$$

$$727 \atop -417$$
___
$$300$$

Bunnies, Bears, and Birthdays © 1991 Fearon Teacher Aids

The Biggest Bear

Written by Lynd Ward
Boston: Houghton Mifflin, 1952

Synopsis

Johnny Orchard is humiliated because his family does not have a bearskin as proof of a courageous hunt. But after Johnny meets and befriends a young bear cub, his perspective changes.

Introduction

Ask children what wild animal they would like to tame and keep as a pet. Ask children to think about some problems that might arise from having a wild animal in captivity. Explain to children that in the story Johnny ends up with a huge bear as a pet. Encourage children to listen closely as the story is read aloud to find out how Johnny feels about the bear and what he decides to do with it.

Critical-Thinking and Discussion Questions

1. Johnny Orchard felt humiliated because no one in his family had ever killed a bear. The Orchards did not have a bearskin to hang on their barn. Why do you think this humiliated Johnny? What does humiliated mean? Would you have felt humiliated if you had been Johnny? Why or why not? Have you ever felt humiliated?

2. Many of the men in the story had shot bears. Do you think this is right? Why do you think the men shot the bears? Can you think of another way to deal with the problems bears might cause rather than shooting them?

3. Johnny enjoyed having a bear for a pet, but the bear soon became too big to keep. How do you think Johnny felt when he had to take the bear back into the woods? How would you have felt? How do you think the bear felt?

4. At the beginning of the story, Johnny could not understand why his grandfather had not shot the bear that he met in the woods one day. Do you think Johnny better understood his grandfather's actions at the end of the story? Why or why not? Do you think Johnny will ever shoot a bear? Why or why not?

5. Do you think the bear will be happy in a cage at the zoo? Why do you think the men put him there?

Creative Writing Starters
Language Arts

If I saw a bear in the woods, I would _____ .
Bears do not make good pets because _____ .
I was humiliated when _____ .

Story Titles
Runaway Bear
Bear Obedience School
The Last Goodbye

Wise Replies
Language Arts

In the story, Johnny's grandfather replied, "Better a bear in the orchard than an Orchard in the bear" when asked why he ran away from a bear he once met in the woods. Ask children to explain what they think Johnny's grandfather meant. Ask children if they think the saying is true. Discuss the meaning of other proverbs and wise sayings:

"Where there's a will there's a way."
"A penny saved is a penny earned."
"A stitch in time saves nine."
"You can't have your cake and eat it, too."
"You can't unscramble eggs."
"Haste makes waste."

Invite students to choose one proverb and write it on the top of a sheet of lined writing paper. Encourage students to write a paragraph explaining its meaning and tell whether they think the saying is true.

Draw a Bear

Art

Give each student a copy of the "Draw a Bear" reproducible on page 47 and a sheet of drawing paper. Invite each student to follow the step-by-step procedure and draw a bear. After some practice, students can add their own features to the bear, color it, and draw scenery surrounding it for a complete picture.

The Big Question

Social Studies

Discuss the treatment the wild animals received in *The Biggest Bear*. Pose the question to students, "Is it right to shoot wild animals or put them in cages?" Divide the class into two groups and set up a debate forum. One side can defend the act of shooting wild animals or putting them in a zoo. The other side can defend the animals' rights to life and freedom. After both sides have been discussed, ask students to brainstorm another solution to the problem Johnny's bear caused in the village.

Make a Map
Social Studies

Johnny traveled to the north, south, east, and west trying to get rid of the bear. Review these directions with the children and then give each child a copy of the "Make a Map" reproducible on page 48. Have children carefully read the description of Johnny's travels and then draw and label each place as they draw their own maps.

Draw a Bear

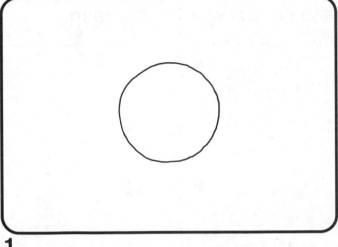

1.

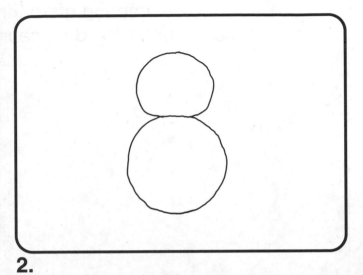

2.

3.

4.

5.

6.

Name _____

Make a Map

Read the description of Johnny's travels below. Draw and label each underlined place in the correct spot on the map.

1. Label your map with the directions *north, south, east,* and *west.*
2. Draw <u>Johnny's house</u> in the center of the map.
3. Johnny walked west from his house to <u>Old Lumber Road</u>, which was past <u>Baldwin's hill</u>.
4. Johnny went east from his house to <u>Blueberry Bluff</u>, which was past <u>Watson's hill</u>.
5. Johnny went south from his house to a <u>lake</u> and then rowed out to <u>Gull's Island</u>.
6. Johnny went north from his house to a part of the <u>woods</u> he had never been before. There were no roads there.
7. Put an X on your map to show where you think the <u>zoo</u> might have been.

Bunnies, Bears, and Birthdays © 1991 Fearon Teacher Aids

The Biggest Bear

Shadow Bear

Written by Joan Hiatt Harlow and illustrated by Jim Arnosky
New York: Doubleday & Company, 1981

Synopsis

George is an Eskimo boy who lives where the nights are sometimes very long. He listens to his father tell stories of a giant, white polar bear as tall as five men. Tarrak, a polar bear cub, lives in a snow den near the ocean. His mother tells him tales of a great hunter as tall as five bears. George and Tarrak meet unexpectedly in the climax of this Arctic story—or at least their larger-than-life shadows meet.

Introduction

Ask children if they have ever been frightened by something they saw. Ask children if they have ever realized that what they saw was not really what they thought it was. Display a plastic spider and show children that at first glance, it may look frightening. Point out that after they realize that it is only a toy, it is no longer frightening. Explain to children that in the story, a little boy and a bear cub are frightened by something they see. Invite children to listen closely as the story is read aloud to find out how the characters handle their fears.

Critical-Thinking and Discussion Questions

1. As George watched his brother leave on a cold, black morning carrying a lantern, he thought about how he would someday walk to school, too. Have you ever watched someone do something and hoped that one day you could do it, too? What?
2. George hoped that someday he would be a great hunter. What do you hope you will be someday?
3. George was very frightened by the huge shadow of the bear. He cried out in a loud voice and ran for home. What would you have done if you had been in George's place? Have you ever felt as frightened as George must have felt? When? What did you do?
4. In what ways were George and Tarrak's experiences similar?
5. George told his family that he scared the great polar bear away. He made himself sound very brave. Was George brave? Did he scare the bear away? Why do you think George told the story the way he did? Have you ever told a story a bit differently than the way it really happened? Why?

Creative Writing Starters
Language Arts

When I am frightened, I usually _____ .
Someday I hope I can _____ .
I feel safe when I am _____ .

Story Titles
The Chance Meeting
Shadow Scare
The Mighty Hunter

Story Spinners
Language Arts

In the long winter nights, George and his family would sit by the fire and tell stories. Sometimes the stories would be "tall tales." Give each child a copy of the "Story Spinners" reproducible on page 52 and a sheet of lined paper. Have each child choose one idea from each of the three spinners (who, what, where) and combine the three ideas to make a complete sentence. Have the children write their sentences at the top of a sheet of lined paper and then write a paragraph or short story expounding on the idea presented in the sentence. Encourage creativity and wild imaginations!

Shadow Suggestions
Language Arts

Have fun sharing some of the many poems, stories, and songs about shadows with your students. *Shadowplay* by George Mendoza is an interesting book showing how to make shadow pictures on the wall with your hands.

Shadow Size
Science

Ask children if they have ever noticed the size of their shadows. Ask them to speculate why George and Tarrak's shadows were larger than they actually were. Divide children into pairs and give each pair a piece of chalk. Take the children outdoors on a sunny day to a spot where they can draw with the chalk on the asphalt or sidewalk. Have each child trace his or her partner's feet and the shadow cast by the partner's body on the ground with the chalk. Have children write their names inside their shadows. Two or three hours later, take the children back outdoors to retrace their shadows. Be sure children stand with their feet carefully placed in the footprint tracing before their partner retraces their shadow. If possible, repeat the shadow tracing again two or three hours later. Explain to the children that the position of the sun in the sky affects the size of the shadows. Ask children what position they think the sun might have been in when George and Tarrak saw their very large shadows.

As Tall as Five
Math

George said the polar bear was "as tall as five men." Tarrak's mother told Tarrak of a hunter that was "as tall as five polar bears." Give students practice in estimation by asking them to compare the height of different objects. Display a chalkboard eraser and then ask students to look around the room and find something they think would be "as tall as five erasers." Invite children to measure some of the suggestions using the eraser. Display another classroom object such as a book, a pencil, or a paper clip and repeat the activity.

Story Spinners

Choose one idea from each spinner. Combine the three ideas to make a silly sentence.

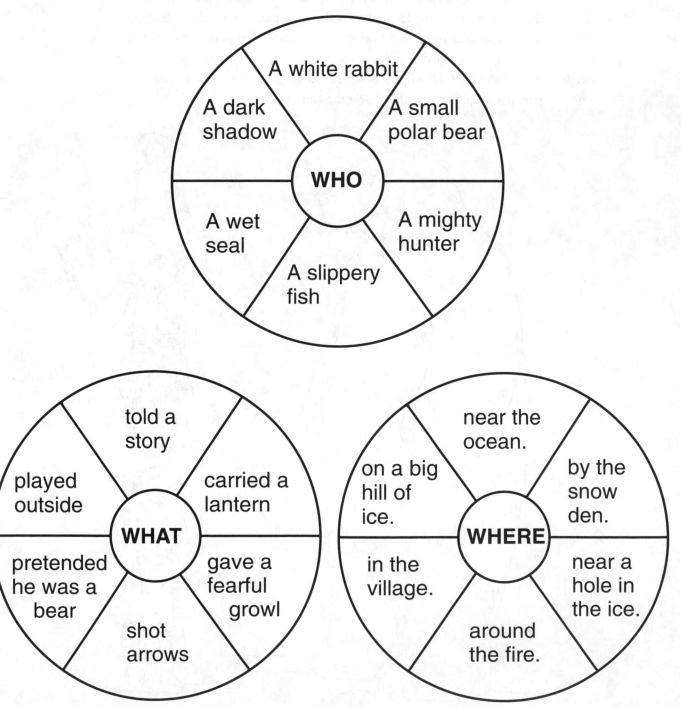

Shadow Bear

The Bear's Bicycle

Written by Emilie Warren McLeod and illustrated by David McPhail
Boston: Little, Brown and Company, 1975

Synopsis

The author carefully outlines safe bicycle-riding procedures, such as walking a bike across the street, steering around broken glass, and staying to the right. Meanwhile, the artist adds a touch of humor by illustrating a huge, happy-go-lucky bear doing just the opposite.

Introduction

Invite students to imagine that today has been declared a "no rule" day and that any school rules that they have been asked to follow can be broken today. After students imagine the great things they anticipate doing in a school with no rules, encourage the students to speculate about why rules are made and if there might be any problems if rules are not enforced. Point out that many rules are made for safety. Invite students to listen carefully as the story is read aloud to find out about some important bicycle rules and what might happen if the rules are not followed.

Critical-Thinking and Discussion Questions

1. Every afternoon, the little boy went bicycle riding. Why do you think he did that? Is there something you do every afternoon? Do you do it because you like to or because you are told to?
2. What are some of the rules for safe bicycle riding that the little boy always remembered? Do you ever go bicycle riding? What rules do you follow?
3. How would you describe the little boy's bicycle ride? How would you describe the bear's bicycle ride? What made the difference in their two experiences? Which ride would you rather have taken? Why?
4. How do you think the people whom the bicyclers met along their journey felt about the bear and his actions? What would you do if you saw a bear on a bicycle coming towards you?
5. Which bicycle rider are you most like—the bear or the little boy? Why? Which one would you rather be like?

Creative Writing Starters
Language Arts

When I ride my bicycle, I _____ .
My favorite thing to do in the afternoon is _____ .
Rules are important because _____ .

Story Titles
How to Fix a Flat
Look Out!
Ridiculous Rules

Bicycle Safety Rules
Language Arts and Art

Ask children to recall some of the safety rules the little boy mentioned in *The Bear's Bicycle*. Encourage each child to choose one important bicycle safety rule to illustrate on a 12" x 18" sheet of construction paper. Have children divide the sheet of paper in half and draw themselves following the rule correctly on one side of the paper and a bear (or other animal of their choice) ignoring the rule on the other side of the paper.

Bicycle Citation
Language Arts

Discuss some of the bear's unsafe bicycle riding practices mentioned in the story. Ask children what happens to adults when they do not follow the rules when driving a car. Discuss the terms *citation, offender,* and *offense.* Remind children that when rules are broken, a consequence often follows. Ask children to name some of the offenses the bear committed and what action they think should be taken. Give each child a copy of the bicycle citation reproducible on page 57. Have children pretend they are police officers and complete the top portion of the citation form. Collect the forms and redistribute them randomly. Have children pretend they are judges and decide on an action to be taken as a consequence for the offense described on the form. Select volunteers to read some of the completed forms aloud.

Build a Bike
Art

Give each child a copy of the "Build a Bike" reproducible on page 58. Invite children to cut out the bicycle parts and glue them on another sheet of paper to "build a bike." Encourage students to add safety features, accessories, and decorations. Children can draw a picture of themselves riding the bike to complete the picture.

Hand Signals
Social Studies

The little boy in *The Bear's Bicycle* used a hand signal to indicate to those around him that he was making a right turn while riding his bicycle. Review this signal with the children, as well as the signal for making a left turn. Ask children if they can think of other hand signals that they have seen or used. Point out that hand signals are used in other instances also. Referees use hand signals at sporting events. Some people use hand signals known as sign language. Find a resource book on dactylology at your local or school library. Teach the children how to fingerspell by learning the hand sign for each letter of the alphabet.

_____ Municipal Court

■ Bicycle Citation Division ■

Date _____

Offender _____
(bear's name)

Address _____
(street)

_____
(city)   (state)

Offense _____

_____

_____

Due to appear in court on _____
(date)

Citation issued by _____

Badge number _____

Action taken _____

_____

_____

Judge _____
(signature)

The Bear's Bicycle

Build a Bike

Carefully cut out the bicycle parts. Glue the parts on another sheet of paper to "build a bike." Add safety features, accessories, and decorations. Draw a picture of yourself riding the bicycle.

rear wheel

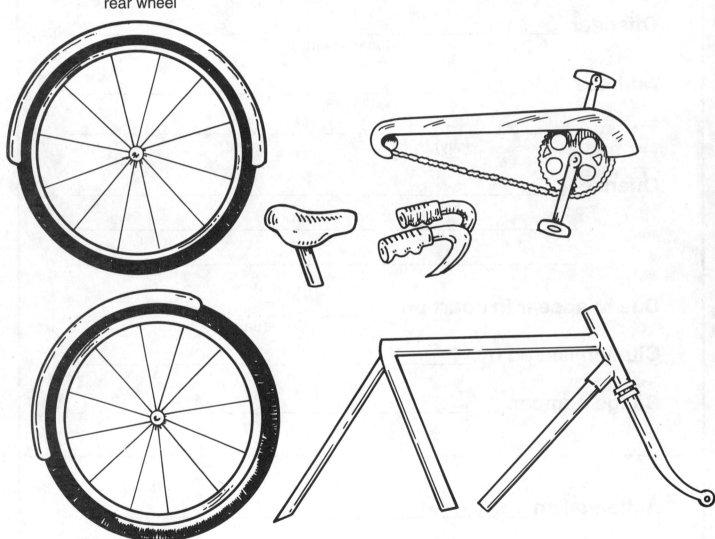

front wheel

Safety Features	Accessories
headlight	basket
reflectors	rearview mirror
kickstand	speedometer
bell or horn	

The Bear's Bicycle

Bunnies, Bears, and Birthdays © 1991 Pearon Teacher Aids

Corduroy

Written and illustrated by Don Freeman
New York: Viking Press, 1968

Synopsis

Corduroy sits quietly on the toy department shelf waiting for someone to give him a home. A little girl named Lisa uses all the money in her piggy bank to purchase Corduroy. Corduroy and Lisa give each other the gift of friendship.

Introduction

Ask children if they have ever searched for something they really wanted to have. Encourage children to tell what they were searching for, how long it took to find it, and if they were happy if and when they got it. Explain to children that in the story, Corduroy, a stuffed bear, and a little girl are in search of something. Invite children to listen closely as the story is read aloud to find out if Corduroy and the little girl find what they are searching for.

Critical-Thinking and Discussion Questions

1. At the beginning of the story, Lisa was very disappointed when her mother said that she could not buy Corduroy. Corduroy was equally disappointed that he would not have a home. Have you ever felt disappointed like Lisa and Corduroy? When?
2. When Corduroy realized that he was missing a button on his overalls, he tried to fix it so that people would be more attracted to him. Have you ever liked or disliked someone because of how they looked? Do you think the way a person looks on the outside affects who they are on the inside? Why or why not?
3. Corduroy tried to replace his missing button by pulling one off a mattress. Can you think of another way Corduroy could have gotten a button? How? If you were Corduroy, what would you have done?
4. The first thing Corduroy saw when he woke up one morning was Lisa's warm smile. What do you think Corduroy was thinking at that moment?
5. Corduroy and Lisa were both very pleased with their new friendship. What are some things you think Corduroy and Lisa will enjoy doing together in the future? What do you enjoy doing with your friends?

Creative Writing Starters

Language Arts

My friend and I like to _____ .

When I go to the toy department, I look at _____ .

I would like to save my money to buy _____ .

Story Titles

My New Friend

The Escalator Escape

Fuzzy Brown Ears

A New Discovery

Language Arts

"Quite by accident he had stepped onto an escalator—up he went! 'Could this be a mountain?' he wondered." Corduroy made a new discovery when he went in search of a new button. He had never ridden an escalator and did not know what it was. Encourage children to think of a time when they made a new discovery. Invite several children to share their experiences with the class. Encourage children to express the emotions they felt (fear, amazement, wonder, excitement).

Bear Cinquain
Language Arts

Ask children to describe Corduroy's looks and actions. Invite children to speculate about how he was feeling throughout the story. Encourage children to describe some aspects of Corduroy's personality and to use as many descriptive and colorful words as possible. Explain the elements of a cinquain:

first line—one-word title

second line—two words describing the title

third line—three words telling about the action of the title

fourth line—four words telling about the author's feelings about the title

fifth line—one word restating the title

Choose a topic and practice writing a cinquain together as a class. Give each child a copy of the "Bear Cinquain" reproducible on page 63. Encourage children to write their own original cinquains about Corduroy.

Corduroy
Art

Reproduce the bear pattern on page 64 on brown construction paper for each child. Use the "Overalls Pattern" on page 65 to cut out a pair of overalls from corduroy fabric for each child. Invite children to cut out their brown bears and glue on the corduroy overalls. Give each student one button to glue on the bear's overalls and encourage children to add details with crayons or markers.

Shopping Spree
Math

Give each child a copy of the "Shopping Spree" reproducible on page 66. Be sure each child has a variety of color crayons. Ask children to color the items on their copies of the reproducible by listening as you read the following directions—one at a time:

1. Draw a ring around the toy that you could buy with three quarters.
2. Color the toy that costs more than the truck yellow.
3. Color the two toys that cost the same amount purple.
4. Color the toy that costs 50 cents more than the bear brown.
5. Put an X on the toy that costs twice as much as the doll.
6. Color the toy that costs two dollars less than the giraffe pink.

Bear Cinquain

_____

1-word title

_____

2 words to describe the title

_____

3 words to describe the action of the title

_____

4 words describing your feelings about the title

_____

1 word about the title

Overalls Pattern

Cut a pair of overalls from corduroy fabric.

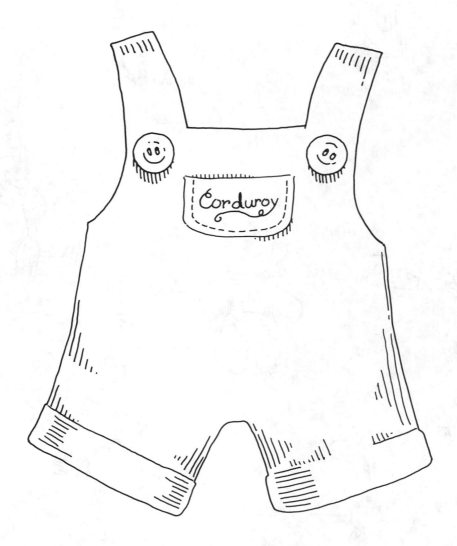

Shopping Spree

Listen carefully to the directions before you color each toy.

Corduroy

Good as New

Written by Barbara Douglass and illustrated by Patience Brewster
New York: Lothrop, Lee & Shepard, 1982

Synopsis

Grady reluctantly allows his cousin K.C. to play with his most prized possession—his stuffed bear. Grady's worst nightmare comes true when he realizes that K.C. has mistreated his bear and buried it in the sand. Grady doubts that his Grandpa has the ability to fix the bear as "good as new," but with ambivalent feelings, allows him to try.

Introduction

Show children an old dirty penny and a new shiny penny. Ask children if they think the old penny could ever again look as "good as new"—like the shiny one does. Explain to children that in the story a little boy named Grady hopes that something he owns can be as "good as new" again. Encourage children to listen closely as the story is read aloud to find out if Grady's hope becomes a reality.

Critical-Thinking and Discussion Questions

1. Grady trusted his Grandpa. He relied on him to solve his problems and he thought he could fix anything. Do you have a family member or friend that you feel this way about? Who?
2. Do you think Grady's parents should have let K.C. play with Grady's bear? Why or why not? Do you think Grady was being selfish by not sharing his bear with K.C.? What would you have done?
3. Do you have a toy or stuffed animal that you consider to be your most prized possession? What is it? What would you do if it got ruined? Would a new one be acceptable to you, or would you want the old one fixed as Grady did?
4. Grady wondered if his Grandpa would fix the bear the right way. Do you think Grandpa ever wondered if he were doing the right thing? How do you think Grady would have felt towards his Grandpa if he were not able to fix the bear as "good as new?"
5. What did Grandpa and Grady decide was the solution to prevent K.C. from damaging the bear again? What do you do to keep your possessions in good condition?

Creative Writing Starters
Language Arts

I would be very sad if anything ever happened to my _____.
When I let my friends play with my toys, I always _____ .
I would like to fix _____ so it would be as good as new.

Story Titles
Mr. Fix-It
Never You Mind
Are You Sure?

Can You Fix It?
Science

Ask children to recall the steps Grandpa took to repair Grady's bear. Ask children to name some items that have needed repair around their homes. Display some tools, such as a hammer, screwdriver, tape, or needle and thread and ask children how the tools could be used to repair something that is broken or torn. Give each child a copy of the "Can You Fix It?" reproducible on page 69. Have the children cut out the square pictures of broken items and the circular tool pictures. Give each child a 9" x 12" sheet of construction paper and invite children to match each broken item with a tool that could be used to fix it and glue the pairs of items side by side on the sheet of construction paper.

Evaporation Evidence
Science

Ask the children how long they think it took for the bear in the story to dry while it was hanging outdoors on the clothesline. Ask the children why they think Grandpa removed the stuffing before he washed the bear. Conduct an evaporation experiment to help children see the reasoning behind Grandpa's actions. Cut four 12" square pieces of fabric. Sew two of the pieces together leaving a 3" hole to add some stuffing. Place the stuffing between the two pieces of fabric and then sew up the 3" hole. Sew the other two pieces together without any stuffing between them. Explain to the children that the stuffed piece of fabric will represent the bear with the stuffing left in and the other two pieces will represent the bear after the stuffing has been removed. Soak both pieces in a tub of water. Squeeze them out and hang them outdoors. Invite children to observe the pieces of fabric as the day progresses to find out which one will dry fastest. Explain the principle of evaporation as you discuss the results. Ask the children to evaluate Grandpa's methods after seeing the experiment results.

Name _____

Can You Fix It?

Cut out each picture. Match each broken item with a tool that you could use to fix it.

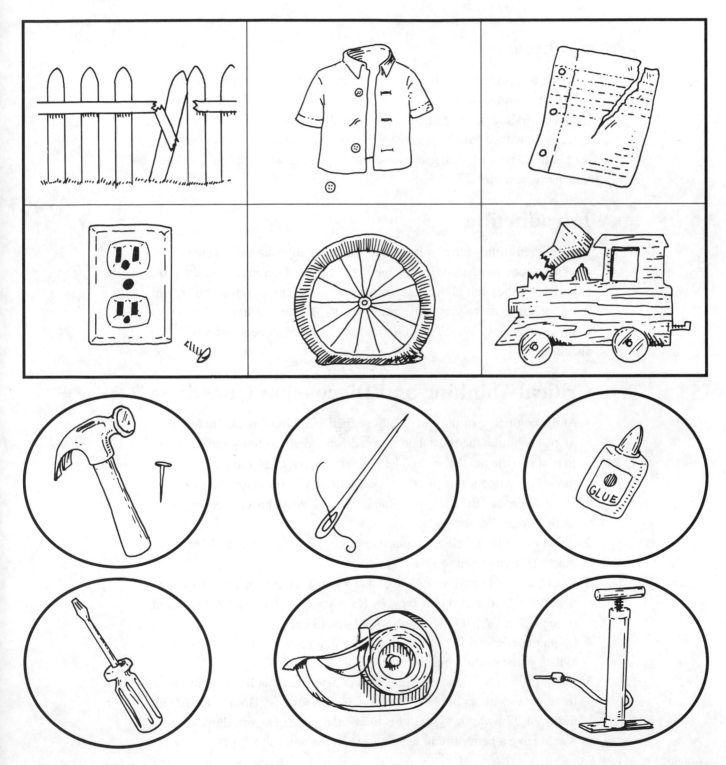

The Bear Who Had No Place to Go

Written and illustrated by James Stevenson
New York: Harper & Row, 1972

Synopsis

Ralph was a circus bear. He loved the cheering crowds, the big tent, and traveling by train. One day Ralph is fired and finds himself with no place to go. After finding life in a big city and a small town undesirable, Ralph meets a rat named Frank who shows him life in the woods. In the woods, Ralph meets new friends, learns new ways of living, and realizes that he now has a new home.

Introduction

Ask children if they have ever moved to a new home, started a new school, or experienced another major change in their lives. Encourage children to express how they felt about the change. Explain to children that the bear in the story has to make some changes in his life. Invite children to listen closely as the story is read aloud to find out how Ralph deals with the changes.

Critical-Thinking and Discussion Questions

1. At the beginning of the story, Ralph experienced loneliness. He felt all alone each time the roustabouts took down the circus tents and prepared to move to the next stop. And he felt very lonely when the circus train moved on without him after Mr. Doll told him he no longer had a job. Have you ever felt lonely like Ralph? When? Why did you feel so all alone? What did you do?

2. Ralph rode his bicycle from place to place. How do you usually get to places that you want to go to?

3. After Ralph was told he no longer had a job at the circus, he got a job delivering groceries on his bicycle. Have you ever had a job? What kind of job was it? What kind of job would you like to have?

4. Ralph experienced life in a big city, in a small town, and in the woods. Which place would you best like to live? Why?

5. Ralph made new friends in the woods and decided that he liked living there. How will his life be different in the woods compared to his life in the circus? In what ways will his life be the same? Do you think a bear would have a better life in the circus or in the woods? Why?

Creative Writing Starters
Language Arts

I would like a job at the circus doing _____ .
If I could choose anywhere to live, I would like to live _____ .
I feel lonely when _____ .

Story Titles
The Job Search
Center Ring at the Circus
The Long Winter Nap

Ralph's Adventure
Language Arts

Give each child a copy of the "Ralph's Adventure" reproducible on page 73 and two sheets of white drawing paper. Have children stack the two sheets of drawing paper on top of each other and fold them once lengthwise and once the other way to make an 8-page booklet. Have children trim the long, folded edge to separate the pages and put two staples on the short, folded end. Children can write "The Bear Who Had No Place to Go" on the front page. Have children cut the sentences apart and glue one on each page of their booklets to retell the story in the correct sequence:

1. Ralph rode a bicycle in the circus.
2. One day, Mr. Doll told Ralph that they didn't need him anymore.
3. Ralph went to the city, but it was too hot and noisy.
4. Ralph went to a small town and got a job at a grocery store.
5. Ralph met Frank, the rat, who took him to the woods.
6. Ralph met many new animal friends.
7. The animal friends presented the Big Woods Circus.

Children can add illustrations to their booklets.

Circus Sign-Ups
Language Arts

Ralph's new friends presented the "Big Woods Circus" to make
Ralph feel at home. The beaver juggled acorns, the possums swung
from tree branches, and the squirrels did a flying act. Divide children
into groups of five or six and encourage them to organize and perform
their own circus acts. Give the groups several days to prepare and
then plan a performance date. Ideas may include magic tricks, acro-
batics, and clown acts. Read the story *If I Ran the Circus* by Dr. Seuss
to the children to serve as an inspiration for some unique circus acts.

Place to Go
Art

Ralph experienced many different environments as the story pro-
gressed. He started out in a circus, rode his bicycle to a big city, took
a job in a small town, and finally ended up in the woods where he
seemed to be the happiest. Ask children what they think would be the
perfect environment for themselves. Discuss the advantages and
disadvantages of living in an environment with a cold climate, warm
climate, lots of people, few people, and so on. Have each child bring a
cardboard shoebox from home to make a diorama depicting the
environment he or she would most like to live in. Encourage children
to gather a variety of 3-D materials to make the dioramas. Extend the
art lesson into other curriculum areas. Invite children to write a
paragraph describing the environment they chose. Or, open a discussion explaining the difference between natural and cultural environments.

Animal News
Science

Ask children to recall all the woods animals mentioned in the story
and make a list on the chalkboard.

rat	chipmunk	possum
raccoon	owl	woodpecker
deer	beaver	owl
turtle	frog	squirrel
skunk	bear	

Put children in pairs or groups of three and invite them to choose one
animal to research. Provide books, encyclopedias, and magazines.
Encourage each group to find out three important facts about their
chosen animal that they think their classmates don't already know.
After the research is complete, invite each group to share their information with the class.

Ralph's Adventure

Cut the sentence strips apart. Put them in the correct order to retell the story of *The Bear Who Had No Place to Go.*

The animal friends presented the Big Woods Circus.

Ralph met Frank, the rat, who took him to the woods.

Ralph rode a bicycle in the circus.

Ralph went to a small town and got a job at a grocery store.

One day, Mr. Doll told Ralph that they didn't need him anymore.

Ralph went to the city, but it was too hot and noisy.

Ralph met many new animal friends.

Lyle and the Birthday Party

Written by Bernard Waber
Boston: Houghton Mifflin, 1966

Synopsis

Feelings of jealousy stir inside Lyle the crocodile as he joins in the fun at Joshua's birthday party. Why can't the party be for him? As the jealousy intensifies, Lyle becomes so sad and moody that his family decides he must be sick. After being admitted to the hospital, Lyle finds the perfect cure for his unwanted emotions.

Introduction

Ask children if they have ever been in a bad mood and to express what put them in a bad mood. Encourage children to tell what they do to put themselves in a better frame of mind. Explain to the children that in the story, Lyle the crocodile is in such a bad mood that he begins to feel sick. Invite children to listen closely as the story is read aloud to find out what causes Lyle's bad mood and what finally cures him.

Critical-Thinking and Discussion Questions

1. Lyle was jealous that the birthday party was for Joshua and not for him. By the time the party was over, Lyle was in a dark, dreadful mood. Have you ever been jealous? What made you feel that way?

2. Lyle did not want to be jealous because it felt awful. In fact, he tried to smile and cover up how he really felt. Have you ever tried to cover up how you really felt? When?

3. No one understood why Lyle was feeling so sad and gloomy. How might the situation have been different if Lyle had told his family why he was feeling so bad? Have you ever had a hard time understanding why a friend of yours was grumpy or sad? How did you treat your friend? Were you impatient or did you try to help your friend feel better?

4. Mrs. Primm finally decided to call the zoo to get some advice on how to help Lyle. Would you have done the same thing? How do you help your friends when you know they are feeling bad?

5. Lyle moped around the house after Joshua's party and then ended up in the hospital because he was feeling so bad. But Lyle finally found a way to rid himself of his jealous feelings. What did he do? Do you think Lyle's idea will work for you next time you feel jealous or sad? Why or why not?

74

Creative Writing Starters
Language Arts

I feel jealous when _____ .
When my friend feels sad, I try to help by _____ .
I feel good about myself when I _____ .

Story Titles
The Imposter
Classroom Crocodile
Green All Over

Emotion Collages
Language Arts and Art

Hold up a sheet of green construction paper and ask children what they think of when they see the color green. Green is often the color associated with jealousy. It is often said that a person may be "green with envy." Other colors are often associated with emotions, too. For example, people are said to be "blue" when they are sad. When a person is "seeing red," he or she is angry. Hold up other colors of construction paper and ask children to name the emotions the colors make them think of. Encourage children to choose one emotion and a color that they think represents that emotion. Invite each child to make a color collage using only the chosen color. Children can use bits of paper, 3-D objects, such as buttons or yarn, and paint, markers, or crayons. After the collages are made, give children the opportunity to share with the class why they chose their colors, what emotions the colors represent, when they most often feel the emotions represented, and the best way to deal with these emotions.

Lyle, the Crocodile Puppet
Art

Give each child a paper lunch sack, a copy of the "Crocodile Puppet" reproducible on page 77, and two 5" x 10 ½" pieces of green construction paper. Have children color the bottom of the bag pink and then refold the end of the bag so that both sides are flat and the same length. Children can glue the green construction paper on the front and back of the bag to make a green crocodile body. Have children cut out the eyes and teeth from the reproducible page and color the eyes. Children can fold the eyes and teeth on the dotted lines to form tabs and glue the tabs in place on their crocodile puppets. Children can draw two nostrils with a black marker or crayon.

Diagnosing Diseases
Health

Introduce the term *symptom*. Ask children to name some of the symptoms Lyle had that indicated he was not feeling well.

> Lyle sulked.
> He was not hungry.
> He moped around the house.
> He didn't want to do anything.

Introduce the term *diagnosis*. Ask children what diagnosis they would have given Lyle after becoming aware of his symptoms.

Ask children to name some of the instruments doctors and nurses use to diagnose problems (stethoscope, thermometer). If possible, take the children on a tour of a hospital or doctor's office to familiarize them with some common diagnostic instruments and procedures.

At Your Service
Social Studies

The help of many community workers was enlisted to diagnose and cure Lyle's ailment. Ask children to recall the helpers mentioned in the story:

zoo worker	ambulance attendants
doctor	lady in the hospital office
telephone operator	nurse

Invite children to name other workers in the community and to tell how they help others. Lyle himself became a helper at the end of the story. Encourage children to think of ways that they can help their classmates, family, or friends. Ask children to speculate about what job they might like to have when they grow up and to tell how it would be of service to others in their community.

Crocodile Puppet

crocodile eyes

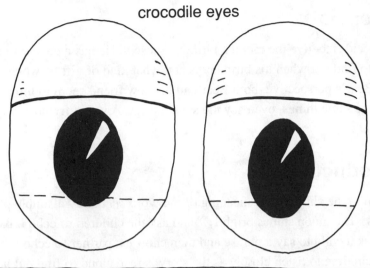

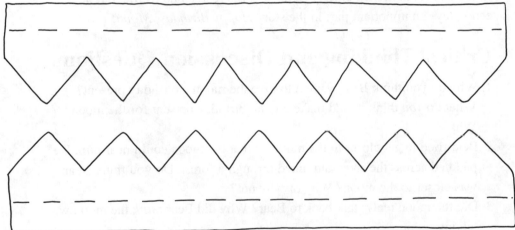

crocodile teeth

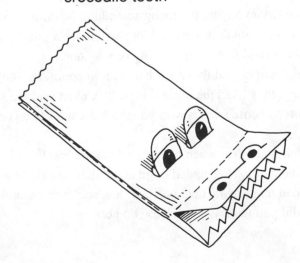

Happy Birthday, Moon

Written and illustrated by Frank Asch
New York: Prentice-Hall, 1982

Synopsis

Bear decides to give the moon a birthday present. He has a chat with the moon to find out when his birthday is and what kind of gift he would like. From Bear's perspective, both Bear and his new friend seem to think alike, enjoy the same things, even say the same things. A warm friendship quickly develops.

Introduction

Explain to the children the meaning of the word *echo*. Say a simple phrase, such as "The moon shines brightly," and ask the children to echo it back to you. Ask a child to say a phrase and then choose a partner to echo it back. Invite children to listen closely as the story is read aloud to find out how an echo plays an important part in the story *Happy Birthday, Moon*.

Critical-Thinking and Discussion Questions

1. Why do you think Bear wanted to give the moon a birthday present? What do *you* think would make a good birthday present for the moon? Why?
2. Bear tried to get closer to the moon so that the moon could hear him. He paddled across the river and hiked through a forest. Do you think Bear was closer to the moon? Why or why not?
3. Did the moon really talk back to Bear? Why did Bear *think* the moon was talking to him?
4. Bear had a hard time deciding what to get the moon for a birthday gift. Bear ended up buying the moon something he himself would like to have. Do you think it is a good idea to choose a gift for a friend that you yourself would like to have? Why or why not?
5. Bear thought he and the moon had a lot in common. They had the same birthday, they liked the same things, they even said the same things. Do you often choose friends who you think are a lot like you? Why or why not?
6. Bear felt really bad when he realized that he had lost his birthday present from the moon. He decided to go and talk to the moon and tell the moon what had happened. Have you ever lost something that was given to you? How did you feel? What did you do about it?

Creative Writing Starters
Language Arts

My favorite birthday present is _____ .
If I could talk to the moon, I would ask _____ .
I would like to wear a hat that would make me look like a _____ .

Story Titles
The Case of the Broken Piggy Bank
The Moon and Me
The Alarming Echo

Reach for the Moon
Language Arts

Bear tried to get closer to the moon by paddling across the river, hiking through the forest, and then standing on a hill. Ask the children if they think Bear was really any closer to the moon. Remind children that astronauts have actually landed on the moon using a rocket to get them there. Encourage children to think of imaginative and creative ways or actual ways of reaching the moon, such as being shot out of a giant sling shot, jumping off a super-charged trampoline, or riding in a rocket. After generating some ideas with the class, give each student a sheet of lined writing paper to write a paragraph telling about his or her idea.

Moon Hats
Art

Give each child a large yellow construction paper circle to represent the moon. Provide children with glue, scissors, and various colors of construction paper and encourage them each to create an original-looking hat for their moon. Display the moons and hats on a bulletin board entitled, "Happy Birthday, Moon."

Sound Waves
Science

Bear thought the moon could talk to him, but in reality the moon's replies were actually just an echo of Bear's own voice. An echo is a sound we hear bouncing off some object, like a wall of a canyon, for example. When a noise is made, sound waves travel through the air in all directions. When the sound waves first reach our ears, we hear the sound. When the sound waves hit some large object, they bounce back and may reach our ears a second time, thereby producing an echo.

Drop a pebble in a shallow dish of water. Invite students to observe the series of waves that travel outward from the point where the pebble entered the water. This wave action demonstrates how sound waves travel in all directions from the point of origin. Sound waves can travel through the air, through water, and through a solid. The words we speak travel through the *air* to a listener's ear. Sonar is an example of a detection device that uses sound waves traveling through *water*. A sonar sends out a sound and receives echoes back. Give children the opportunity to test the ability of sound waves to travel through a *solid* by making a string telephone. Give each pair of children two paper cups, two paper clips, and a length of string. Have each child punch a small hole in the bottom of his or her paper cup with a pencil and thread the string through from the outside of the cup to the inside.

Have each child tie the end of the string to the paper clip so the string does not pull back through the hole in the cup. Have each partner hold his or her cup and stand a distance apart with the string taut. One partner can speak into the cup while the other holds the cup to his or her ear to listen for the message as the sound waves travel through the string.

A Letter to Amy

Written and illustrated by Ezra Jack Keats
New York: Harper & Row, 1968

Synopsis

Peter wants very badly to invite Amy to his birthday party, although he wonders what all the other boys will think. He writes Amy a special invitation, mails it, and then waits anxiously on the day of his party hoping Amy will attend.

Introduction

Ask children if they have ever worried about what their actions might cause others to think about them. Explain to children that the little boy in the story is worried about what his friends will think of him if he invites a girl to his birthday party. Invite the children to listen closely as the story is read aloud to find out how Peter's friends react to the situation.

Critical-Thinking and Discussion Questions

1. Peter told his mother that he was mailing an invitation to Amy rather than inviting her to his party in person because "that way it's sort of special." What do you think he meant by that? Do you think there was another reason why he mailed the invitation?
2. Peter wondered what the boys would say when they saw a girl at his party? Have you ever wondered what your friends would think of something you did? What?
3. How do you think Amy felt being the only girl at the party? How would you feel if you were the only girl or boy at a party? Have you ever felt like you stood out as being different from everyone else? Why did you feel that way?
4. What do you think Amy thought about Peter when he knocked her down and grabbed the letter? What could Peter have done to prevent Amy from crying and feeling so badly?
5. Everyone gave Peter advice about what to wish for when he blew out his birthday candles. But Peter made his own wish. What do you think he wished for? If your birthday were today, what would you wish for?

Creative Writing Starters
Language Arts

I would like to write a letter to _____ and say _____ .
At my birthday party, I want to _____ .
When I blow out my birthday candles, I will wish for _____ .

Story Titles
The Flying Letter
The Spoiled Surprise
My Best Birthday Wish

Party Invitation
Language Arts

Peter forgot to write some important information when he was making the invitation to mail to Amy. He had to quickly add the information on the back of the envelope. Ask children to think about the important information that should be included on a party invitation, such as the time, date, and place of the party, the type of party, and who is giving the party. Make a list on the chalkboard. Many invitations include an R.S.V.P. (abbreviation for the French words *Respondez s'il vous plait*) and although Peter doesn't include it, you might want to discuss its meaning and purpose. Give each child a copy of the party invitation reproducible on page 84. Invite children to fill in the information for their very own party, add designs to fit the theme of the party, and then fold each invitation so that it opens like a book.

Post Office Play
Language Arts

Peter's job of delivering the invitation to Amy was finished after he put the letter in the mailbox. However, the letter still had some traveling to do before Amy received it. Take children on a tour of a post office so they can become familiar with mail delivery procedures, such as postmarking, sorting, and delivering. Discuss the importance of addressing envelopes correctly, including the use of proper zip codes. Provide children with play props such as pens, pencils, stamps, ink pads, sorting boxes, envelopes, mail pouches, unopened junk mail, and scales. Encourage children to dramatize postal employees at work.

Party Hats
Art

Give each student a sheet of colored construction paper. Have the children draw a party hat and decorate it using crayons, markers, yarn,

or scraps of construction paper. Encourage children to be creative and make a tassel for the top of the hat. After the hat is decorated, children can cut out and punch two holes on each side of the hat near the bottom edge and thread a string through each hole. Children can tie the strings under their chins and wear the hats.

Date: _____
Time: _____
Place: _____
Given by: _____

party! ☆

_____

You are
invited to a

A Letter to Amy

The Half-Birthday Party

Written by Charlotte Pomerantz and illustrated by DyAnne DiSalvo-Ryan
New York: Clarion Books, 1984

Synopsis

Daniel decides to give his 6-month-old sister a half-birthday party. He asks each guest to bring half a present. In all the excitement of planning the party, Daniel forgets to get a half present of his own. While each guest tells the story about his or her gift, Daniel searches frantically for an idea. His gift turns out to be the most clever of all.

Introduction

Ask children if they have ever had trouble deciding on a gift to bring to a birthday party. Ask if anyone has ever forgotten to bring a gift and to tell how they felt. Explain to the children that the little boy in the story forgets to get a special gift for his little sister and then when he remembers, he has trouble deciding what to give her. Invite the children to listen closely as the story is read aloud to find out what gift Daniel gives his sister.

Critical-Thinking and Discussion Questions

1. Daniel was very excited when he saw his younger sister pull herself up and stand for the first time. Can you remember a time when you did something for the very first time? What did you do? How did you feel?
2. Daniel was very proud of his sister. In fact, he was so proud of her that he wanted to do something special—so he planned a birthday party. Have you ever planned something really special for a member of your family or a friend? What did you plan? If not, who would you like to plan something special for and why?
3. If you received the invitation to Katie's party and were told to bring half a present, what would you bring?
4. When Daniel realized that he had forgotten Katie's present, he gulped, his heart started thumping, and he felt hot and sweaty. Have you ever experienced these symptoms of nervousness? When? What made you feel that way?
5. When Daniel was asked if he knew all along that he would give Katie a half-moon, he said, "It's half true." What do you think he meant by that? Have you ever told a half-truth? Why? What was it?

Creative Writing Starters
Language Arts

My half birthday is in the month of _____ .
If I had to bring half a present to a party, I would bring _____ .
I would like to plan a special party for _____ because _____ .

Story Titles
The Crazy Quote
Best is Last
The Half Truth

Quote Collection
Language Arts

The definition of a quote in the story is "when somebody else said it first." Grandpa recited the following two quotes:

"The best things come in small packages."
"The best things come last."

Recite some of the following quotes and ask children to explain their meanings.

"A bird in the hand is worth two in the bush."
"Don't count your chickens before they hatch."
"The early bird catches the worm."

Encourage children to invent some original ideas for quotes that convey messages that they feel are true.

Half-Drawings
Art

Give each student a 9" x 12" sheet of white construction paper. Have the children place the paper vertically on their desks. Invite children to draw one large, simple picture in the center of the paper. Large objects such as an apple, clock face, person's face, gift box, tree, or house work best. After the drawing is complete, have children fold the papers in half vertically, open them up, and cut them in half on the fold line. Invite children to exchange half of their drawings with another classmate. (The other half will not be used and can be thrown away or kept for another purpose.) Children can glue the half-drawings they receive on a new 9"x 12" sheet of white construction paper. Encourage students to complete the pictures by drawing the missing half. This activity can also be used in conjunction with a lesson on symmetry. Students replicate the half-drawings (designs rather than pictures would work best) they receive on the other side of the paper to look like a reflection.

JAN.   FEB.   MAR.   APRIL   MAY   JUNE

JULY   AUG.   SEPT.   OCT.   NOV.   DEC.

Half-Birthdays
Math

Make a list on the chalkboard of the twelve months of the year from January to December. Help children figure out when their half-birthdays would be. Make a class bar graph on the chalkboard to represent the class half-birthdays.

Moon Phases
Science

Ask children what shape the moon is. Some children may think that the moon varies in shape over the course of a month. Help children to understand that the moon does not actually change its shape . Explain the cycle of the moon and the terms *new moon, waxing crescent, half moon, full moon,* and *waning crescent*. When the moon is waxing (getting larger), the rounded, curved side will be on the same side as the curve in the letter "D." When the moon is waning (getting smaller), the rounded, curved side will be on the same side as the curve in the letter "C." At the time of a "new moon," we cannot see any of the moon at all. Give each student a copy of the "Moon Phases" reproducible on page 88. Invite students to color the moon pictures and cut them out. Help children glue the pictures in the correct boxes to accurately depict the six phases of the moon.

Moon Phases

Cut apart the worksheet on the dotted line. Color each picture of the moon yellow. Color the box with no moon in it black. Cut out each box below the dotted line and glue the boxes in the correct places to show the phases of the moon.

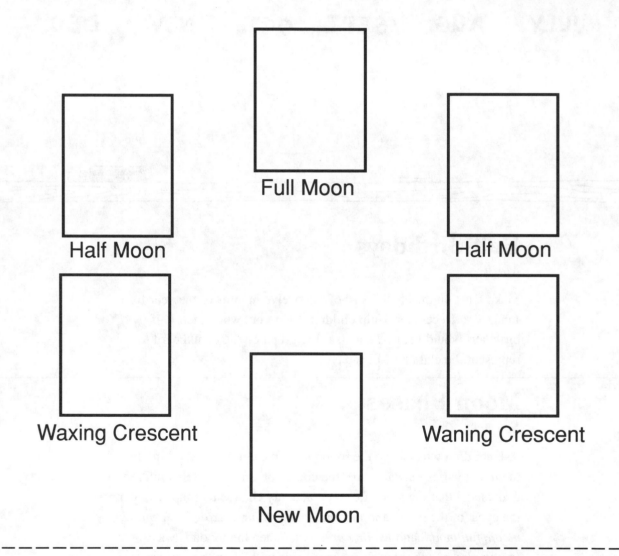

Full Moon

Half Moon

Half Moon

Waxing Crescent

Waning Crescent

New Moon

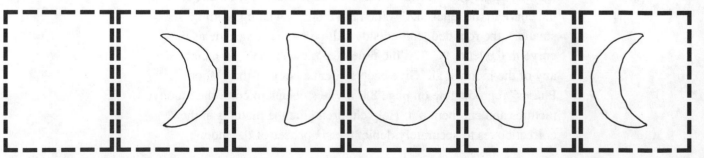

Birthday Presents

Written and illustrated by Eugene Fern
New York: Farrar, Straus & Giroux, 1967

Synopsis

Joseph received a very special gift from his grandfather. The gift was not something that could walk, talk, or jump like the gifts children around him had received, but Joseph's gift would last forever. Joseph shares his gift with those around him and with you, the reader.

Introduction

Ask children to name some things that, in their estimation, last a long, long time. Ask children what their oldest possession is and to explain why they think it has lasted so long. Explain to children that in the story, Joseph receives a birthday present when he is just a little boy. He still has this present when he is a grandfather. Invite children to listen closely as the story is read aloud to find out what the birthday present is.

Critical-Thinking and Discussion Questions

1. The gift Joseph received could not be wrapped or touched, but was enjoyed by many. What are some other gifts that cannot be wrapped or touched that you could give as a present?
2. Of all the gifts described in the story (a monster, a set of dishes and a stove, a truck, a doll, a kangaroo, and a song), which one would you most like to receive? Why?
3. When the children first heard about the gift Joseph received, they laughed. How do you think that made Joseph feel? Has anyone ever laughed at you? How did you feel?
4. How do you think the children felt about Joseph's gift after their gifts had been ruined?
5. Joseph's gift lasted a very long time. In fact, he still had it when he was a grandfather. What gift of yours has lasted the longest? What gift lasted the shortest amount of time? What type of gifts do you think last the longest?

Creative Writing Starters
Language Arts

The best gift I ever received was a _____ because _____ .
A gift I received that has lasted the longest is _____ .
The gift I would most like to give to someone is _____ .

Story Titles
Crushed, Broken, and Spoiled
The Song That Lived Forever
The Best Gift Ever

Long-Lasting Gift
Language Arts

Joseph learned a new song that his grandfather gave to him. By storing it in his memory, the song became a gift that would last forever. Encourage children to give themselves a long-lasting gift by memorizing a new song, poem, story, or joke. Invite students to share their gifts with the class by reciting them on a designated performance date.

Rhythm Repeat
Language Arts

The song in the back of *Birthday Presents* has a simple melody and rhythm. Children should be able to learn it quickly. Present some other melodies or rhythms to increase children's listening and sequencing skills. Clap a simple rhythm and ask children to repeat it. Begin with a simple rhythm, such as three even claps followed by two quick claps. Increase the difficulty and length of each rhythm to make the task more challenging. Vary the activity by using a series of words or numbers and ask children to repeat the pattern back verbally. Or use a xylophone and play a simple three- or four-note melody and ask a volunteer to repeat it back.

Sing Me
Music

Teach the song "Sing Me," found in the back of *Birthday Presents,* to the children. Encourage children to add hand motions and body movements to accompany the lyrics.

Happy Birthday, Dear Duck

Written by Eve Bunting and illustrated by Jan Brett
New York: Clarion Books, 1988

Synopsis

When Duck's friends give him a swimming suit, a yellow chair to float in, and some suntan oil, he thanks them, but wonders how he will use his new gifts since there is no lake or sea nearby. The last guest to arrive at Duck's party brings a gift that solves the mystery.

Introduction

Ask children to tell about one of the best gifts they ever received. Ask children if they have ever received a gift that they weren't sure they could use or weren't sure they really liked. Explain to the children that in this story, Duck receives some gifts that he isn't sure he can use. Invite children to listen carefully as the story is read aloud to find out what gifts Duck receives and if he finds a use for them.

Critical-Thinking and Discussion Questions

1. Duck thought that he would not be able to use the gifts he received from his friends. Have you ever received a gift that you didn't think you could use? What was it? Were you able to use it?
2. Duck's friends sat around impatiently waiting for the last guest, Tortoise, to arrive. Have you ever had to wait for someone or something? How did you feel? Have you ever been late and left someone waiting for you? Do you think it is important to be on time? Why or why not?
3. Suppose Tortoise had been the *first* guest to arrive and Duck opened his gift before he opened the gifts from his other friends. How would the story have been different?
4. Duck had corn crackle cakes, grasshopper cookies, and polliwog shakes at his birthday party. What kind of treats would you like to have at your birthday party?
5. For his birthday, Duck got "a day filled with friends who liked him a lot." If you could gather all your friends together for a day filled with fun, what would you plan to do?

Creative Writing Starters
Language Arts

At my birthday party, I would like to _____ .
The perfect present for my friend, _____ , would be a _____ .
I get impatient when I have to wait for _____ .

Story Titles
The Mystery Gift
A Day Filled with Fun
Usually Late

Poetry Party
Language Arts

Read the story aloud again, but do not say the last word on each page.
Ask children to fill in the rhyming word to complete each sentence.
Divide children into groups of three students each. Assign each group
a rhyming word pair from the story such as wait/late, sea/me, or air/
wear. Invite each group to brainstorm and list as many other words that
rhyme with their word pair as possible in two minutes. Ask a spokes-
person from each group to read the list. Have the class help discard
any words that do not rhyme or are not real words. Encourage groups
to use the edited lists of rhyming words to write an original, rhyming
birthday invitation.

Birthday Bash
Language Arts

Give each student a copy of the "Birthday Bash" reproducible on page 94. Discuss the foods that were served at Duck's party (corn crackle cakes, grasshopper cookies, and polliwog shakes). Discuss the fun that Duck's friends planned for the party (swimming). Encourage students to imagine that they are planning a birthday for a friend of theirs. Invite students to list some games they would like to play with their friends and some foods they would plan to serve. At the bottom of the worksheet, encourage students to write a detailed description of how to play one of the games on their list or to write a complete recipe describing how to make one of their foods.

Plastic Pool Play
Science

Show children the picture in *Happy Birthday, Dear Duck* that shows Duck and his friends splashing about in the plastic pool. Encourage children to notice who or what is under the water and who or what is on top. Discuss sink and float objects and their properties. Divide children into pairs and give each pair a plastic bowl filled with water, the "Sink or Float" reproducible on page 95, and the test objects listed on the reproducible. Encourage children to test each object to see if it sinks or floats and to mark their responses on the worksheet.

Climate Contrast
Social Studies

Duck and his friends lived in a desert where there were no bodies of water, such as ponds, lakes, streams, or oceans. Duck first thought it a bit impractical for his friends to give him such gifts as a swimming suit and a scuba mask. Give each child a copy of the "Climate Contrast" reproducible on page 96. Point out each location on a globe or world map. Discuss the climate and natural environment of each place. Invite students to list one item under the suitcase column that they would definitely take with them if they were planning a trip to that location. Ask children to list one item under the suitcase with an X on it that they would *not* take because it would be impractical or useless. For example, if a student were planning a trip to Hawaii, he or she would want to take along a swimming suit, but it would be impractical to take along a pair of mittens.

Name _____

Birthday Bash

Pretend you are planning a birthday party for a friend of yours. Make a list of games and goodies you would plan to have at the party.

Games	**Goodies**
_____	_____
_____	_____
_____	_____
_____	_____
_____	_____

Explain how to play one of the games on your list or write a recipe explaining how to make one of the goodies.

_____

_____

_____

_____

_____

_____

_____

_____

_____

Happy Birthday, Dear Duck

Sink or Float

Test each object to find out if it will sink or float by putting it in your plastic pool of water. Write an **S** after each object that sinks. Write an **F** after each object that floats.

1. pencil _____

2. crayon _____

3. cotton ball _____

4. scissors _____

5. bar of soap _____

6. piece of chalk _____

7. penny _____

8. piece of paper _____

9. rubberband _____

10. marshmallow _____

Name _____

Climate Contrast

Think of one item that you would take with you if you were
planning a trip to each location listed below. Write the name of the
item under the suitcase. Think of one item that you would
not take with you because it would be impractical or useless.
Write the name of the item under the suitcase with an X on it.

Hawaii   _____   _____

Mt. Everest   _____   _____

Sahara Desert   _____   _____

Arctic Circle   _____   _____

Happy Birthday, Dear Duck